Izabela Luiza Jahn

Radical Practice Peace of Mind

Imprint

Bibliographic information of the German National Library:
The German National Library lists this publication in the German
National Bibliography; detailed bibliographic data are available on the
Internet at http://dnb.dnb.de.

© 2021 Izabela Luiza Jahn (German Edition)
© Cover photo: Izabela Luiza Jahn
© 2022 Izabela Luiza Jahn (English Edition)

Production and publishing house: BoD - Books on Demand,
Norderstedt

Bibliografische Information der Deutschen Nationalbibliothek:
Die Deutsche Nationalbibliothek verzeichnet diese Publikation in der
Deutschen Nationalbibliografie; detaillierte bibliografische Daten sind
im Internet über http://dnb.dnb.de abrufbar.

© 2022 Izabela Luiza Jahn
© Umschlagfoto: Izabela Luiza Jahn
Übersetzung ins Englische: deepl.com & Izabela Luiza Jahn

Herstellung und Verlag: BoD – Books on Demand, Norderstedt
ISBN 9783755786139

MIX
Papier aus verantwortungsvollen Quellen
Paper from responsible sources
FSC® C105338

Until you actually live your values and insights, what you think doesn't really matter. It only becomes significant when you act on it.

AKRASIA IS NOT A WONDERLAND

An old coaching adage is, "If you can't apply it yourself, make it an advice." The world is full of knowledge about "what is good for us" and of people who have that knowledge in their heads, but then turn around and do the exact opposite.

The ancient Greeks had their own word for this phenomenon: akrasia. It's easier to grasp than "acting against one's better judgment. We know this: "I'm not eating these chips. No way. "Crunch, smack." Bag empty... And boom: guilty conscience and self-loathing. And now that it all doesn't matter anyway: where was the chocolate?"

Exactly, self-control is considered the antidote. A clear plan for self-improvement, with goals and discipline as means of salvation. The six-pack as proof of performance and self-esteem. This then leads, among other things, to high-tech packed uphill and smile-avoiding cyclists who doggedly complete their optimized training plans and then post the evaluation begging for likes on Facebook or Insta. Social media in particular is full of the perfect bodies, eyebrows, workouts and meals optimized in their gluten content, the perfect morning routine and the perfect life anyway. Everything is planned, has a goal and must bring a benefit, otherwise it's all nothing. It's all about the YOU, and the advertising slogan for it certainly includes a you, your, for you and a bunch of emotions and hyped experiences, because that sells best. You too can have the perfect lifestyle, body and experiences (with our product). Is that really doable? Can we be perfect if we just pull ourselves together and shop the right stuff? Probably not, when there is the yo-yo effect and supposedly 90% of all New Year's resolutions fail, and relationships always revolve around the same problems. In many countries people have hardly any money to spare, but many supposedly salvific products. There are things from which there seems to be no escape. Siren song that always leaves us smashed against the same cliff.

Weaknesses. Everyone has them. Not everyone likes to admit it. Not everyone sees them either. And then comes the well-known cliff... it's almost reassuring. Everyone must have a weakness; it is not said for nothing. Hehe.
Yes quite funny. Only it was supposedly Einstein who said so aptly that "it is madness to do the same thing over and over again but expect different results." It wasn't Einstein, of course. It just makes the saying sound more legitimate and weighty in a world that confuses famous names with authority and competence in a special field. The saying is still true, just by the way....

But then what's the problem? If perfection is not possible, then weakness is okay, right?
The problem is that we strive for perfection where it is unattainable or obsolete, and we squeeze both eyes tightly shut on grandiose weaknesses. We polish the facade and sweep the dirt inside instead of getting rid of it and wonder why happiness and fulfillment do not materialize. But what really brings happiness?

Apparently, it's not the good school degree, not the diploma, and not the car. Nor is it the house - and it's not the family. And it's certainly not the promotion, and it's not even the six-pack. At best, all of this briefly creates a high mood, and afterwards everything is just as gray as before. Or worse, because now you have to do everything to keep the six-pack maintained or you'll fail and fail...

We like to believe it very much that "if only xy, then I will be furiously and wishfully happy." But practice teaches us that this a. is not true, even if things turn out as you liked and b. is always "something" that does not go as intended. So you can only lose that way. Everyone who is older than twenty knows from experience that the "Once I have xy, then I'll be happy" song is not true. It's just that we like to believe it - perhaps for lack of an alternative?

How to win? Have no expectations? But still keep demands?
Is it even possible to win? Is there one solution, or is it all very complicated and still individual?

My favorite thinker says: "Happiness is our natural state. Happiness is the natural state of little children; they own the kingdom until the stupidity of society and culture infects and corrupts them. To attain happiness, you don't have to do anything, because happiness cannot be attained. Do you know why? Because we already have it. How can you attain what you already have? But then why don't you experience it? Because you have to lose something first, and that is your illusions. You don't need anything extra to be happy; on the contrary, you need to lose something. Life is easy, life is fun. It's just hard on your illusions, ambitions, greed, desires." [1] So you have to lose to gain. But what exactly are we supposed to lose?

TAKE OUT THE TRASH

Strictly speaking, we need to get rid of the obstructive garbage from our head. There is only one small problem, an original sin if you will, which keeps us from paradise, and which we unfortunately have factory-built into us by the manufacturer. As mammals, we come into the world very underdeveloped and are existentially dependent on the care of our parents, and programmed to do everything to please them and receive their affection in order to actually survive. And by everything, I really mean everything. The parents are God in the child's universe and it does everything to fit in. Even if you have/had loving parents, they have their own limitations and deformations that have been passed on to you because you have been raised in certain ways (by your parents consciously and also unconsciously) accordingly. As a rule, you are not brought up to develop your full potential and to be happy, but at best to "have it good"-meaning to function well in society and to have a financial livelihood. And that means as a child you are supposed to be well-behaved and obedient - so you are brought up to function according to certain ideas. These are not necessarily yours.   And this is still the best case. The more serious your parents' problems with themselves or one another are, in short, the more dysfunctional your family is, the more you have a big problem: because in order to survive, you adapt to a completely sick system to the maximum, while still telling yourself that you are to blame, because unfortunately children relate everything to themselves. Not only is there no happiness there and no fostering appropriate and fair to the child, but the "perfect" adaptation to a dysfunctional system is what happens instead. This causes many permanent damages. What was experienced in childhood really leaves deep tracks and forms the personality and social skills of the child:

"As early as the 1940s, within the framework of the attachment research established by John Bowlby and Mary Ainsworth, the insight was corroborated that the first years of life are crucial in the maturation of this "social brain". This is in the context of the early childhood attachment experience with the primary caregiver, i.e. usually - but by no means necessarily - with the mother. On the one hand, the infant and toddler experience the benefits of care from the caregiver, and this generates a primordial trust. At the same time, the emotional-communicative interaction slowly differentiates the child's initially still diffuse emotional world. The way in which the caregiver interacts with him or her imprints their emotional world on the child, at least in part. This applies especially to dealing with stress and strain, such as temporary separation from the mother, the ability to wait for rewards, to curb spontaneous impulses, to resolve conflicts without violence, or to develop an idea of how others feel and think - in other words, everything that belongs to basic social skills. "[2]

Where it goes wrong, it has a devastating effect and permanently impairs personal development:

"However, this presupposes that the person providing care, i.e. usually the mother, has appropriate competencies herself. If these are not present or not sufficiently present, for example due to the mother's own lack of attachment experiences, traumatization through maltreatment, abuse or severe strokes of fate, then these deficits imprint themselves in a disastrous way on the psyche and personality of the young child. They also form the basis of later psychological disorders, including poor attachment skills in adolescence and adulthood. There is then a greatly increased risk that a depressed mother will pass on her illness to her children through her behavior.

The consequences of such negative influences in early childhood can now be detected in the brains of adolescents and adults using various neurobiological methods. This is usually done by measuring the amount of certain substances relevant to the psyche (neurotransmitters, neuropeptides, neurohormones) and combining them with the results of functional magnetic resonance imaging. This shows that, due to early childhood damage, those parts of the brain are particularly affected that have to do with dealing with stress, with self-soothing, impulse inhibition, bonding and empathy. However, it is also noted that such deficits in both brain and behavior usually disappear if good alternative attachment experiences are made within about two years.

[...] Actually, it's never too late to do so, although improving one's state of mind is increasingly difficult to achieve the older the person is."[3]

This partly explains why it is so difficult to change fundamental things permanently and sustainably. In my last book, I wrote that it is "my basic insight is [...] that we don't want to admit certain things:

1. That it all lies in childhood (and traumatic difficult experiences in adulthood, if applicable).

2. That we are so imbued with it that it doesn't occur to us in everyday life that there might be something wrong with our perception.
3. Or that we think our problems are so special that the "easy methods" don't help anyway
4. Whereby this is also only an ingenious attempt to evade responsibility for oneself
5. And to avoid having to change anything
6. For we fear the unknown more than we fear the known pain."[4]

We think of ourselves as rational and reason-driven beings, yet we only rationalize our behavior in retrospect for our supposed benefit. Even cognitive insight - if it succeeds in breaking through the repression and exposing beliefs - is not enough. For it are the emotions that control our behavior and these are deeply ingrained in us and can be reactivated with old behavior patterns in a fraction of a second. Especially during stress, we fall back into old coping strategies, and in addition, the burden of stress is also felt much more massive, one is virtually punished twice. Where one needs calmness and composure the most, this is gone, and you regress much faster into childlike behavior patterns.

Our childhood also shapes our choice of partner; we don't necessarily look for the partner who is really good for us, but one who gives us the familiar feelings from childhood that we think are love. These, if some theories are to be believed, have not changed since then, so we have a very childish and immature idea of "being loved". So if you come from a dysfunctional family, you will inevtable look for the partner who will recreate with you the dynamics of your childhood and give you the familiar charge of pain. [5]

What does all this mean for our question? As a reminder, can you really take out the trash? Can you put it all behind you? Properly, thoroughly, definitively?

Yes, but on the one hand you are afraid to apply what you have perhaps even recognized as right, because it can mean confronting yourself, standing there alone and starting from scratch. And on the other hand, you become a toddler again through your emotions in the partnership, or in dealing with people important to you, and everything is back to the way it was. Nothing changes, or small changes go down in vehement friction with time, or they go down because you fall back into old behavior patterns out of habit. We also live in a society that calls us to do "what feels good to you" and thus be "authentic." However, this means that you can simply follow your whims, impulses and emotions, and thereby also be a "big immature child" or even an "authentic asshole" who hurts others and simply acts out in an unreflective and inconsiderate (possibly also autodestructive) manner. Miłosz Brzezinski said so beautifully in an interview, "Authenticity is not a value in itself." This is absolutely true, and also explains why, despite all individualism and supposed "authenticity," we do not really arrive at a happy and meaningful life.

We lack not only true self-understanding, but also morality. Morality in particular has become quite unpopular in recent decades. It is regarded as a dusty relic of the world religions, as a rigid small-minded rule, which our progressive enlightened world does not need.

Is it true? In an interview, Jordan Peterson says very aptly in response to the question of whether there is no other truth than only the scientific one:

"That's not true, because what scientific truth tells you is how things are. But it is the real religious truth that tells you how you should behave."[6]

Steven Covey also has this idea, which he summarizes under the concept of principles: "These are natural laws, part of the fabric of every civilized society in history. [...] These principles are part of almost every major enduring religion, as well as of enduring social philosophies and ethical systems. They are evident, and can be easily verified by anyone. *It is almost as if these principles or natural laws were*

part of the human condition, of human consciousness, of human conscience.
They seem to be present in all human beings, regardless of social conditioning
and loyalty to them, even though they may sometimes be suppressed or
numbed. "[7]

So it's time to dig inside and ask yourself: what values do I have?
Which ones are important to me? And the most important question: do
I pay lip service to them, or do I live by them? What does a valuable,
meaningful life look like for me? Do I live it?

"This is how you should act: You should act in such a way that things
are good for you, as they are for someone you care about, but they
have to be good for you in a way that is also good for your family, and
they also have to be good for you and your family in a way that is also
good for society and maybe even good for the general environment
and the environment and the world [...] and that's now, next week, a
year from now, and ten years from now. "[8]

RADICAL HONESTY

It's crucial to be honest with yourself. It is extremely difficult to
actually see your own weaknesses (I don't mean the flirtatious crap
you say in job interviews) but the ones that keep falling in front of
your feet, making life difficult. How to crack the repression, and to
search in the primordial mucus for beliefs etc. etc. and to transform
them, I have explained in detail in the previous book[9] and described
various techniques useful for doing this there. Here in a nutshell: yes,
it comes from the childhood, how you were shaped (consciously,
unconsciously), it must be recognized and accepted, only then you can
change something. Everything you push away and don't want to see is
exactly what is in the way. Call things by their names. Before this

becomes a nice-spirited air act, check whether there is a difference in what you think of yourself and how you then behave in certain real situations. Perhaps you have accepted yourself, but when dealing with people important to you (partners, parents, and superiors) you feel you always have to do something special to earn love, recognition and acceptance? These are two pairs of shoes. But that means that you only really value yourself while pondering on your couch.

Do you have boundaries? Do you show them? Or do you smile kindly all the time, no matter what is done to you, and bend because you can't stand conflict, or you fear rejection... There is no shame in that, but as I said, you can only change what you admit to yourself. And changing is still a challenge in itself.

As long as you are determined by external things, and do not decide from your innermost being (which is built on clear foundations and thoughtfully made decisions), others or circumstances will decide for you. This may seem comfortable, just letting yourself drift, and explains why so many people do not question themselves and avoid introspection like the devil avoids holy water. But that's the biggest problem: "Whenever we think the problem is "out there," that thought is the problem. We give what's out there the power to have control over us."[10]

If one follows Covey's argument, there are basically two kinds of people (by whatever means they have become that way), *but they lead diametrically different lives as a result:*
"It means that we as human beings are responsible for our own lives. Our behavior is a function of our choices, not of given conditions. We can subordinate our feelings to values. We have the initiative and the responsibility to shape things. The ability to subordinate an impulse to a value is the essence of a proactive person. Reactive people are driven by feelings, circumstances, conditions, or their environment. Pro-active people get the drive from their values - carefully considered, selected, and internalized values."[11] It also follows that really only the non-reactive people are given "their" life. The others get if at all then perhaps by happy coincidence one with which they are satisfied. If you

are reactive, you are the plaything of many vicissitudes and if necessary you still see yourself as a victim. "[People] feel more and more like victims with no control over their lives and destinies. They blame their situation on forces outside themselves, other people, circumstances, even the stars."[12]

It is true, however, that "whether a problem is directly, indirectly, or beyond our control, [...] we [hold] the first step toward its solution in our hands. Our habits, the way we take influence, and our ways of dealing with problems that are beyond our control are all within our own sphere of influence."[13] Viktor Frankl recognized (and he did this as a prisoner in a concentration camp!) that "the last of human freedoms [consists] in the choice of attitude toward things." He elaborates that: "between stimulus and reaction [lies] a space. In this space lies our power to choose our reaction. In our reaction lie our development and our freedom."[14]

No matter what life brings us, we are responsible for how we decide to deal with it and whether we grow or harm ourselves and/or others as a result. Ideally, the decision is based on clear, unambiguous values that are always valid for you and that you fill with life accordingly - in other words, on your integrity.

RADICAL ACTION

Until you actually live your values and insights, what you think doesn't really matter. It only becomes significant when you act on it. But that is very difficult, isn't it?

How many people do you know who say they want to live healthy and eat healthy, but simply "forget" it as soon as they get an appetite for something unhealthy? How many who say they want nothing more than to find a loving partner and that family is important to them, but who then "tinder" through the world wondering "why love doesn't work out"?

It is said so well "You get what you repeat" and exactly so it comes. You can think and wish what you want, but if you act differently, you will be determined by your actions in the long run. So, to stay with the last example, you teach yourself to keep interpersonal contacts superficial and functional, and to have shallow, meaningless sex that does not allow for deep intimate connection (this only succeeds in consistent relationships that you also maintain well).[15] Furthermore, commitment and reliability is rather also not a criterion that is lived in our example, but in a relationship these qualities are of particular importance. Your actions take you away from what you actually want to achieve, and over time affect your ability to live the kind of relationship you supposedly want. Quite a high price to pay for that bit of "fun", isn't it?

Here it happens perhaps insidiously, and long time unnoticed in the effects. Whereby the effects of our actions are usually delayed. That's why doing the right thing in the "here and now" is so unattractive. In the "here and now", other things bring the short-term reward, but when looked at more closely, this is a Trojan horse. It's harder to do without the more reactive you are (and this can vary in different areas of life, so don't get too excited too soon, or look down on other people too hastily). A lot of it is not so obvious, like actually wanting to diet and still eating cake every day. What is it with you? An important question in this context is what kind of people do you surround yourself with? Whether "peer group effect, or the 5 person rule according to Jim Rohn, which says that you are the average of the five people you spend the most time with, or as a Polish proverb that says that you become like the people you associate with[16] - it boils down to the same thing - your company influences you and how you are or become,. And this will happen, even if you tend to believe, that it does not influence you. Do you know how to turn an ordinary person into a torturer? Really quite simple, the most prominent examples are Milgram with his electric shocks, or Zimbardo's prison experiment. So be vigilant and choose wisely what you do and who you surround yourself with. We are much more situational and dependent on our environment for our actions than we would like to admit. Your environment has a lasting influence on your behavior and the values you hold and what else you consider significant and right.

Choose the people - who will influence you with certainty - wisely, because you become like them. This can build us up or pull us down....

THE SIGNIFICANT OTHER

I hope for your sake that there are not too many people whose opinion you seriously value and worry about.[17] Nevertheless, for each of us there is at least one person who can do more in this respect, perhaps even more than he should: the partner.

And there it goes, his problems become yours, and yours are additionally fueled by the partner, as said before, because you look for him "fitting" to your impairments.[18] Your problems are even additionally magnified by it. Even if you really say everything that causes you difficulties to your partner clearly, you will often make the observation that this changes nothing or even intensifies the problems. Why is this so?

There's a brilliant scene in the sitcom Big Bang Theory that explains just that. There, Penny asks Sheldon to tell her something personal about himself. He then tells her that he can't live with the fact that YouTube has changed its rating system, which Penny simply dismisses. To which he responds: "And here's something else you don't know about me: you just hurt me. I open up and confide in you about something that's bothering me, and you react like it is nothingness. It's bad for me, that's what it's all about." [19]

I am convinced there are several reasons for this. The most important one is: it is not your partner's problem, and that means that *it does not cause **him** emotional pain.*
Since it is not his problem/pain, there are *no immediate negative effects or consequences for* your partner. There is *no reason for* the partner to *change anything.*

But you have an external source that feeds your problem permanently. At best, it works the other way around; you consciously or unconsciously feed your partner's problems - precisely because they are not yours, and you don't really understand them and therefore don't take them seriously and deal with them accordingly. Or your problems are even more triggered by his, which in turn reinforces his, creating a negative cycle that is difficult to break.
In the worst case, if both sides do not change anything, the equation will eventually be: partner = problem.

Here I am not talking about toxic people - as in the previous book - but about problems that, to a certain extent, each of us carries with us. But when these add up and the mutual injuries cannot heal because the same mistakes are repeated over and over again, and thus the frustration and perceived helplessness increase, there is an even bigger problem. Out of self-protection, one stops being vulnerable and showing oneself openly to the partner in order not to offer even more surface for attack. With this, however, one also stops being honest with oneself, and this is very big crap, because then one is not congruent for oneself and actually also no longer in relationship with the other person, since he is only shown piecemeal. This hurts oneself the most, almost more than anything else. *I believe that accumulated hurts and the avoidance of open honest communication, as well as the fear of conflict reinforced by fear of loss, poison any originally good relationship in the long run. In my experience, this is exactly what threatens long-term relationships the most and corrodes them in the long run.* Especially because it just doesn't work without vulnerability: "Love and belonging are known to be an indispensable need for everyone, and without vulnerability, you can't feel love and belonging."[20]

The only advantage of an argument in which you yell so that the other person's hair flies off is: for a moment you yourself don't care about the consequences, and you may be honest at all after a long time. The other person can hardly miss the fact that something really really really affects you and that it is a real problem for you. It is only important, when the emotions have subsided, to sit down and then talk honestly and openly in peace. This is when change happens (if at all). At least then both know where they stand with the other. Even if it becomes clear that the limitations of the partner belong to the (here I follow Gottman's choice of words) "unsolvable problems", there are still certain possibilities.

Maybe you realize in an honest conversation that it is rather your partner's limitations, and not ill will, that make life difficult for you, and realize that his behavior says more about him than about you. Perhaps you will learn to evaluate the behavior differently, and to deal with it emotionally different too.

Maybe you learn to deal with it differently in a practical way, or you change your behavior and reactions in certain situations. Perhaps you can work out a partial compromise together that, with some good will, you can both live with, even if the perpetual conflict behind it continues (e.g., on the topic of order, dealing with money, or closeness). Gottman speaks here of a stalemate: "When you are stuck in a stalemate, it just seems impossible to imagine that your difficulties are just a kind of psychological rheumatism that you can learn to live with. But that's exactly how it is. The goal when it comes to overcoming a stalemate is not to solve the problem, but rather to get out of the bind and into the conversation. "The insurmountable conflict will always be a constant issue in your marriage, but one day you will be able to talk about it without hurting each other. You will learn to live with the problem."[21] [...] To do that, you need to go inside yourself and try to split the issue into two categories. *In one you put those aspects of the issue where you absolutely cannot make any concessions without giving up your basic needs or core values.* In the second category, put all the aspects of the issue where you can be flexible because they are not so "hot" for you. Try to keep the second category as large as possible, while keeping the first as small as possible." [22]

But you can live with it only if your problem with the partner does not permanently touch the first category, and exceeds your limits and values. You must clearly indicate this to the partner, and on the one hand protect yourself, on the other hand demand a change from him. If you give in here, otherwise you will hate your partner and especially yourself for betraying your own values. An example from Gottman's book on the subject of loyalty in marriage (this is about a conflict with the in-laws, primarily the mother, but it can be applied to any group of people):
"The only way out of this dilemma is for the husband to support his wife against his mother. This may sound harsh, but it must be remembered that one of the most fundamental tasks of marriage is to create a sense of "we" between husband and wife. So the husband must let his mother know that his wife does indeed come first, [that] she comes before everything else for him. It is absolutely crucial for a marriage that the husband take a clear stance on this matter."[23]

As it has probably already become clear, your partner will not really quickly realize, or even want to realize, that his deficits absolutely require a change. This sometimes takes a lot of time and a certain insight, to recognize, what all is damaged, due to his lack of insight and partial inability to also protect his own boundaries and set priorities. In Gottman's example, „In an attempt to impress his parents, Noel sacrificed togetherness with Evelyn by talking badly about her. Once Noel realized that his desire for approval from his parents was directed against Evelyn and their marriage, he was able to change." [24]

Until that happens, try to see it as a statement not about yourself, but as a statement about your partner's weaknesses and deficiencies. Work on your own weaknesses and deficits. But work: "Many people say that a good marriage has to be "worked for", but unfortunately this is often lip service. And what exactly is meant by this? Every marriage must face certain emotional tasks that the husband and wife must accomplish together in order for the marriage to grow and deepen. These tasks require a great deal of understanding so that both feel secure in them. If these tasks are not fulfilled, then marriage is not a harbor in the storm of life, but simply another storm."[25]

EMOTIONS

In our previous two possibilities, the main difference is that in the good case, one is a plannful creator of one's own life, guided by values, and in the bad case, one is, to a certain extent, an endurer of one's life, driven by circumstances.

As we have seen, there is also this dichotomy in the most important relationship, between an attitude characterized by (self-)security and cooperative openness and, at the other hand, a reaction to external influences characterized by negative experiences, anxiety and pain. What causes this? In the previous chapter the keyword has already been mentioned: Needs. More precisely, the fulfillment or deep frustration and neglect of these needs. Maslow has already shown that we as humans have so-called deficit needs, i.e. where a deficiency must be eliminated (food, sleep, security, housing, income, social needs) until we can even advance to the higher levels of growth needs (recognition, validity, self-actualization - in short: personal development). Klaus Grawe has formulated four basic psychological needs that "are present in all people and whose violation or permanent non-satisfaction leads to damage to mental health and well-being."[26] He includes the need for attachment (connectedness), which is about being in intimate meaningful contact with others. The need for orientation and control - that is, for a safe and reasonably reliable predictable environment that allows one's own influence: as well as, internally, the feeling of being able to rely on oneself. Furthermore, the need for self-esteem enhancement or self-esteem protection: this describes the desire to perceive oneself as competent, valuable and valued by others. Last but not least, the need for pleasure and avoidance of unpleasure: the desire to experience pleasant and pleasurable experiences and states and to avoid unpleasant and painful ones as far as possible.

In order to feel happy and be psychologically healthy, every need must be sufficiently satisfied. If this is not the case, we perceive this in the form of inner restlessness, nervousness, negative physical sensations or in the form of feelings such as unwillingness, excessive demands, sadness and fear, but also anger. The fulfillment of our needs goes hand in hand with positive feelings and the feeling of self-efficacy (i.e. proactivity), whereas non-fulfillment is associated with negative emotional states and reactive behavior patterns.

The dichotomy proactive and reactive is also found in our emotional world and it reaches down to the neuronal level (here I will adopt Rick Hanson's terms "responsive" and "reactive" from now on). Hanson, like Grawe, recurs to need satisfaction - in his set-up it is the fulfillment of three basic needs: security, satisfaction, and belonging. He assigns these to three brain structures: the brain stem, the limbic system, and the cortex. The common thread for Hanson is also needs and their fulfillment or non-fulfillment. He says, "There is a widespread assumption in medicine and psychology that how we feel and act - both in terms of the whole life course and in terms of specific relationships - s conditioned by three factors: the *challenges* we face, our *vulnerability to* those challenges, and our strength to meet the challenges and protect our vulnerability."[27] Hansons says, "The brain is a learning organ [...] everything we repeatedly take in, what we sense, feel, want, and think, slowly but surely changes the neural structures of our brain."[28] So beware: shit in - shit out. But there is an even bigger problem: "A few experiences of futile effort are enough to create a sense of helplessness - one of the most important causes of depression - and it takes a multitude of counteracting experiences to restore awareness of one's own capability and sufficiency. One way or another, negative states of mind quickly become negative neural features."[29] This is because bad experiences shrink anything positive, which is further fueled by an evolutionary built-in survival program. In the evolution of living things, it was existentially necessary to notice any sabre-toothed tiger because death was imminent. "Consequently, the brain evolved a built-in negative bias [negativity bias]. This bias first appeared in existential situations that are largely foreign to us today."[30]

It works like this: "First of all, the brain is constantly on the lookout for potential danger or loss. In the course of evolution, animals that were irritable, nervous and suspicious had a greater chance of passing on their genes than more lethargic conspecifics, a fact that has since been woven into the solid structure of our DNA. Even when we're feeling cheerful and relaxed, our brains are always looking for potential danger, disappointment and interpersonal problems."[31] "There are even certain regions in the amygdala that prevent us from getting rid of our fears, which is especially true in relation to childhood experiences."[32] - here it is especially worth examining very critically. In general, we absorb the negative faster, easier and stronger, and negative experiences very quickly create a neural trace of these experiences in the brain (to protect us from them). "Negative moments devalue positive ones to a greater extent than positive ones can ennoble negative ones.[33] [...] in interpersonal relationships, trust is quickly squandered but difficult to restore.[34] In long-lasting close relationships, it takes at least five positive interactions to offset each negative one. People feel comfortable when positive moments outweigh negative ones by at least a three-to-one ratio - preferably higher."[35] So far so good, but the negative weighs more heavily (it is also weighted differently in Fredrickson's 3:1 model) and Hanson himself says, „Over time, the amygdala becomes more receptive to negative messages. [...] So if you feel stressed, tense, lonely or hurt today, you will be all the more receptive to feeling stressed, tense, etc. tomorrow, not to mention the day after next. The negative is potentiated and sets in motion a true vicious cycle."[36]

How strongly this affects you is also conditioned by your disposition, childhood experiences, any traumas and of course also by the current life circumstances, because all of this triggers, depending on what you experience, the fear that ultimately stands behind all negative emotions. De Mello once said so beautifully: "there is only love and fear" - he is right. In human evolution, belonging to the tribe was also of existential importance, because if you renounced your tribe, evolution very quickly renounced you. Cooperation with others, their recognition and belonging to a group were crucial for survival, and even today people do the strangest things to fit in with a group they don't even know - I'm thinking here of Solomon Asch's conformity experiment. I think that very thing (that we were existentially dependent on acceptance and recognition and belonging to others at the time) is the cause of fear of loss, which is stronger the more significant the relationship is to us. Some people could not "live without the other" - which is of course absolute nonsense, but nevertheless feels that way for the person concerned.

This leads us via the need for affiliation ultimately back to the need for security, and to another big problem, which comes to light especially in couple relationships (but also other close and significant ones), and ultimately damages them. Milosz Brzezinski said so beautifully in a podcast, "No one puts up with as much from us as our partner. We would have been fired from our jobs a long time ago if they got to hear what we say to our partner."[37] It's explained by the fact that no one else puts up with so much. And why is that?
There is a very simple bottom line here: in relationships, we become emotionally dependent the closer the relationship becomes and the more meaningful it is to us. If you are bothered by the term emotional dependency, let's call it this: you have given the other person access to your emotions and vulnerability to a degree that other people do not

have. You love this person and want to be loved back, you want to live your life with him and not without him, you are not indifferent to the person, on the contrary, this is the most important person on this planet for you. (Let's remember the evolutionary scheme that you will not survive without others and for this reason you absolutely need to be accepted and liked by them - this is activated then - and thus this existential fear is awakened). This leads to the fear of losing this relationship and to the "softening" of your own boundaries. Especially in the beginning you want it to be nice, forgive a lot from the trust-advance that is still there, and don't want to look like the spoilsport. Then you say something, and the other person doesn't really take it serious (see previous chapter) and then human nature comes through, testing how far one can actually go (like small children sometimes test the limits of their parents) and there it shows: the greater the fear of loss of the other person is, the further one is willing to ignore ones limits unduly. The problem with boundaries is: "Remember that a boundary always refers to yourself and not to the other person. You are not demanding that your partner does something - not even respecting your boundaries, [and here's the thing:] you are setting boundaries to show what YOU will or will not do. Only this kind of boundary is enforceable, because you alone are in control. You [...] allow [your partner], with your behavior, to take responsibility for his own behavior."[38] It's his decision, but it's your choice. But if I'm afraid to enforce my boundaries, it's a trap .... And this, over time, leads to a lack of respect for the partner in the relationship (here's the answer to why we treat our loved ones worse than anyone else - for one thing, because they are the most forgiving out of fear and "love," and because you take them for granted out of habit). The slowly growing inability to communicate, protect and enforce one's own boundaries then leads to negative feelings and a sense of helplessness. And at worst, eventually to hatred for the partner, who allows himself to behave in such ways, and even worse, to self-hatred that we allow someone to treat us this way ...

So it is fear of loss vs. respecting one's own boundaries (the need for self-fulfillment, by the way, appears only after the basic needs, maybe that's why it starts to bother so late that someone doesn't respect our boundaries and we subordinate them too readily at the beginning; Malgorzata Marczewska even says that the strongest human need is now that for closeness, for which we subordinate even the primary needs, and this because it guarantees the preservation of the species) ...

And of course, when you have been married for many years, have three children and two cats, and a house with credit, the question arises: "should I open a can of worms because of this, or give it all up, because my partner sees no reason to change his behavior and keeps crossing my limits? Maybe it will change?" Now counter question, "Why do we think/hope/expect something to get better if we allow it to be bad?" It seems to me that many couples think that some dose of mutual humiliation is part of the relationship, and that somehow the other person has to put up with their partner having their "outbursts" for the sake of the relationship. But no, this is wrong. If your partner's behavior is destructive (e.g., the partner plunges your family into debt, binge drinks, or does drugs, etc.) or is humiliating or violates your moral values, then those are boundaries that need to be protected, because those boundaries are essential to the integrity of the person. In this case of your integrity, it will erode and destroy you from within if you permanently disregard them. Here, your well-being is more important than any relationship, even though this idea may scare you, because this relationship is at least bordering on toxicity in that case. If your partner gives your basic needs and your values a "workout" on a regular basis, predictably countable on two fingers, which shakes them, then you will only know proactive mode from this book. Due to permanent stress (because you are in a state of alarm and your brain anticipates the next "event" thanks to bad experience and negativity bias) you are reactive and it is very hard to get out of it under permanent stress. There is always a thorn in the flesh, which sends out waves of pain, and in this case there are always new confirmations in addition, a real vicious circle is created, from which it is really very difficult to get out.

Because in order to calm down the need for security, which is in a state of alarm, and above all to restore the trust in the partner, it will take a while, even with a one-time misconduct, and above all the counterpart should prevent it "at all costs to commit the same mistake again."[39] However, when a pattern of behavior is predictably repeated, there inevitably comes a point when it is important to ask: "Why am I taking this on? What values is it supposed to serve?" and the answer is: None.

You are just teaching yourself and your partner to act out pathological pain in your relationship." He is not changing anything about his weaknesses, and you are not confronting your fear of loss and hoping for "improvement" by doing nothing, which, what can also be counted on two fingers, simply leads to aggravation. As I explained before, our scripts of "love" are very childish and immature, because that's exactly where they come from, and mostly our "role models" were not good at all. Add to that the "evolutionary-existential misprogramming" that I described here, and you can explain why people so often are no longer themselves in a relationship over time, and do not make rational decisions - because overflowing emotions, no longer guided by reason, take control.

Don't get me wrong: emotions are very valuable in indicating that something is wrong (or just fine). But they don't bring a good solution; they want something to stop immediately - at any cost. This creates, among other things, the "Pathological Pain" that I brought into play earlier: by this I mean, a pain and strain that objectively should not be a part of life, because you "consciously, or out of conscious negligence hurt [or are hurt]"[40] , or when someone humiliates you or behaves shamefully. The pain arises when you refuse to take responsibility for your actions, or demand this from your partner, and bend yourself like a pretzel to fit in because of fear of loss ... In contrast to this is the real pain that life brings: people you love die or depart from your life, your child or partner or you become seriously ill, you lose your job, become a victim of a crime /accident, live in a war zone, or experience a natural disaster - I think the difference is clear.

The first pain you should not tolerate for a minute in your life, with the other you should learn to live as well as possible, and also there look for approaches how your life can still be as fulfilling as possible and happy again. Surprisingly, my impression is that we humans can handle real strokes of fate much better after a phase of processing, while pathological pain is simply destructive (probably because it has no end, and we feel its senselessness inside us, which furthermore intensifies the feeling of helplessness). It is like a swamp that sucks you up and pulls you down. I think this is due to the fact that we transfer the influence to the other person, and we ourselves only react emotionally to his drifting. Pathological pain, as I understand it, puts people into reactive mode. It makes them indirectly give influence about themselves also to other (for the partner) "important" people, oscillating around the people important for him, what ultimately leads to the feeling of being at the mercy of the others. The bitter truth is: that it is so, you do it yourself. You give this person this overriding importance, and subordinate everything to it, including common sense and, in case of doubt, self-respect. And the longer this goes on, the more it turns out that Facebook's saying is true: that if something costs peace of mind, the price is too high.

We allow this because we "love" immaturely, (evolutionarily existentially) dependent and childishly, and accept everything in the name of this "love". Have you ever had the experience yourself, when you decided to renounce such a partner after all, how everything that was once sooo enormously important, and the person(s) around whom you circled in many conflicts, suddenly became completely meaningless, just like the supposedly decisive conflicts? That you even started to forget the names of the (indirectly) affected people, who previously robbed you of sleep? To forget what it was all about? That you simply became indifferent to it? I wish it to you with all my heart, it is very salutary and the proof that it is all a question of the importance you assign to it.

Gottman says in "Die 7 Geheimnisse der glücklichen Ehe" that your partner comes before everyone else (i.e. mom, dad, your own kids, friends, and whoever else is hanging around). As you open up to your partner and allow closeness, making yourself vulnerable, your partner clearly has an influence on your feelings and well-being. However, he also has a great responsibility with it. There are elementary boundaries - esteem (respect), loyalty and morality - that can not be crossed, because otherwise we damage ourselves. In a mature (proactive if you will) love, one knows about the mutual responsibility and wants to grow together with the partner and for oneself, to develop and become the best version of oneself. Mature love makes demands and has a goal that goes beyond mere "keeping" of the relationship, which is about creating something beyond the parties involved and that is good. There is no place here for such a stunted caricature of a "relationship" as I described earlier. Here something wonderful is happening. Pope John Paul II said at Jasna Góra in Poland: "Demand it from yourselves, even if others do not." I would add, "Demand it from your partner as well."

I have described this in such detail because not respecting your boundaries will take you to your limits. Boundaries are elemental to your integrity. Your failure to respect them will catapult you into reactive mode. It will happen very quickly. „All it takes is for us to be anxious or upset, to feel restless, or to be exposed to criticism. This upsets our resting state and triggers the brain's reactive "red" mode. [...] The neural circuits of our ancestors, originally designed to ensure bare survival, now speak up when we have money worries, feel under pressure professionally, or have been given the cold shoulder by another person. The reactive mode is responsible for urgent needs, so it doesn't take care of our long-term needs.[41] We remember, emotions want it done right away, not necessarily well. "At the same time, the negative bias ensures that our memory systems, especially the implicit one, neuronally anchor these experiences. The reactive mode is the neural foundation of all longings (by which I mean a basic sense of lack or restlessness) as well as of sorrow and suffering, which it evokes in us. [...] A red light, in function since ancient times, gives us to understand: Something is wrong! Watch out! [...] And because of our unique ability to maintain states of consciousness independent of external factors, internalized psychological processes keep our stress alive even when the challenges are long gone. As a result, the reactive mode [...] has become the normal state for many people - [due to everyday stress, consumption, and bad news, as Hanson outlines in his example]. This doesn't have to be a feeling that hits us terribly [but imagine that added to the other factors]. [42]

The price for the reactive mode is very high: "The red zone makes us feel bad, shifts the perspective to the negative, and makes learning difficult. It robs us of resources that would have served our well-being and personal growth. It makes us depressed and fainthearted, and makes us resort to unhealthy means of "self-healing", such as: gluttony, alcohol, and drugs, video games and pornography. Meanwhile, the stress responses prevent our bodies from performing long-term rebuilding and repair. The red zone feels bad because it is bad. Its unpleasantness is an unmistakable invitation to leave that area and avoid it in the future.

We should not underestimate the growing influence of reactive experiences. Over a long period of time, depression or other mental illnesses can result."[43]

Nietzsche said so beautifully, "What does not kill me makes me stronger." - I don't know, sometimes we can emerge stronger from crises. But it can also make you feel really bad. That's why it's essential to take care of yourself and the quality of your relationship; otherwise you'll have a problem 24/7.

RESPECT YOURSELF

The "German Society for Emotional Competence" (Deutsche Gesellschaft für Emotionale Kompetenz e.V.) writes on its homepage: "Emotions are the essence of life. Their basic elements are perception, evaluation, motivation and feeling. They are rational in a normative sense: they are an appropriate reaction under given circumstances. "[44] As a rule, the object of emotions is human beings - ourselves or other people. [...] Emotions provide information about our relationship to others and ourselves. Thus, emotions are of social nature. Emotional competence is the ability to deal with ourselves in a protective way and to have successful relationships with others - in private interactions as well as in contacts with colleagues, superiors or customers.[45]

We are not born with emotional competence and the ability to self-regulate emotionally. These include the ability to recognize feelings, to verbalize them, to understand how they arise, to be able to regulate them, to empathize with others emotionally and mentally, and to feel compassion. Here we need good competent role models and appropriate guidance, and here we are only as good as our closest caregivers were, and it applies, like in the German proverb "what little Fritz does not learn, Fritz knows even less...". If your "role models" were themselves emotionally illiterate, and had poor coping strategies, or even your difficult emotions were badly tolerated by them and thus punished, so you have great deficits and probably also difficulties to consciously perceive your emotions, to be able to name them and without false shame to live them out appropriately without being destructive. However, if we rarely (due to lack of competence) consciously control our emotions, we will be controlled by them, especially when things are going badly. They run away with us, and then, as in Plato's analogy of the charioteer of the chariot, it is "over" for our mind. It usually keeps the horses (desires, emotions) in check, but when they run away, it's over. Emotions are also wrong advisors, they want, as already said, that a condition immediately stops. If we only want what first feels pleasant and takes the pressure off us, then the door is open for e.g. addictive behavior, which causes considerable damage in the long run. There is then also no mature basis for decisions.

Stephen Covey writes: "When we fail to develop our own self-awareness and take responsibility [...] in our personal lives, we give other people and circumstances outside our control the power to shape large parts of our lives. We reactively live out the scripts that family, colleagues, other people's schedules, the pressures of circumstance dictate to us - scripts from our earlier years, from our education, from our conditioning. *These scripts are man-made, not shaped by principles.* And they arise from our deep vulnerabilities, our strong dependence on others, and our need for acceptance and love, for belonging and significance and a sense of being important."[46] Covey says, "Whatever is at the center of our lives, it will be the source of our security, direction, wisdom and strength."[47] However, "centers" created from the outside or in response to something (one can be family-centered, money-centered, or enemy-centered, among others) bring great limitations, and allow the influence outlined earlier in Covey's quote. He says; „People cannot live with change unless there is an unchanging core within them. The key to changeability lies in an unchanging sense of who we are, why we exist, and what we value." [48]

We need a creed, a clear statement of who we are, what we aspire to, and the values on which our being and actions are based. We need principles:
"Our security comes from the knowledge that correct principles, unlike centers based on people or things, which are subject to frequent change, are constant. We can rely on them. Principles do not react to anything. They don't get angry and treat us differently; they don't get divorced and run away with our best friend. They don't come after us. They can't pave our way with shortcuts and patent solutions. They don't depend on the behavior of others, the environment, or their fashionable validity. Principles do not die. [...] Even in the midst of people or circumstances that seem to ignore these principles, we can be

uplifted in the knowledge that principles are greater than people or circumstances and that they have triumphed over and over again for thousands of years. More importantly, we know for certain that we can confirm them in our own lives, in our own experiences. [...] Principles are always accompanied by natural consequences. If we live in harmony with the principles, positive consequences arise. If we ignore them, negative. But since these principles apply to everyone, whether they are aware of them or not, the limitation is universal. [...] When we center our lives on timeless, unchanging principles, we create a fundamental paradigm of effective living. This is the center that puts *everything* else in perspective. "[49]

They create meaning and significance and integrity in our lives when, for the sake of other people or circumstances, we don't betray them - and that has to do with self-respect.
Ajahn Brahm said in one of his Friday talks that the greatest obstacle to happiness are our emotions, when they overwhelm us and we don't know how to face them. That they then inhibit our growth, and therefore we should tackle the negative, difficult emotions first, because they block the path to [soul] peace, and as we learned from Hanson, they weigh far more heavily... How do you do that?[50]

Covey advises to write your own personal life statement (constitution). Clear rules that always apply, no matter who or what you are dealing with. Here's an example from relationship initiation, and if the reader finds a Buddhist monk and a management consultant too far from reality as advisors, well, then we'll draw from another barrel: "Mannual" by Steve Santagati. There we read (he has a nice pen, so I'll quote at some length): "I know what it's like to meet a wonderful person when you've had a string of duds. You don't want to lose him or her, so you're overprotective. You concentrate fully on not disturbing the peace. Really bad idea. While you don't have to act like a bull in a china store right away, you should slowly but surely show him or her which points in the relationship are non-negotiable for you. You must not be afraid of losing him if you let him feel your long arm of the law. Every woman should have her own personal ground rules that she never overrides in her search for love. It is already written in the Bible [...], "What good it is for someone to gain the whole world vet forfeit their soul?" You must not put your soul, that is, your most important convictions, at risk. If you don't make the rules too complicated and also abide by them yourself, your love will only grow stronger. If he runs away from you, you've just saved yourself months of love stress. Amen."[51]

So here too, a constitution (rules that protect integrity and peace of mind). And about emotions we read: „Feel with your heart, but make decisions with your mind, remembering your guidelines whenever your heart advises you to do something completely stupid or to sell yourself short".[52] The mind makes the decision according to the rules set. And why, and especially why that's hard: "Because you've got your jackpot right in front of you. You're so close; you're dead certain that very soon he's going to understand your point of view and abide by your rules and treat you with the respect you deserve. Wrong. He won't. He's a dog who's gotten used to jumping on the bed and peeing on the carpet, and now it's too late."[53] Ovid's "Resist the beginnings" sends his regards. "You have to be willing to just walk away if the deal is no good. If you find it hard now, think how hard it will be after months or years of a messed up relationship." [54]

Of course, a constitution does not only apply to the relationship, but formulates bindingly one's own values and moral concepts and intentions as to how one's own life should be structured and oriented. This is best done in writing. On the one hand, you don't have to question yourself over and over again and decide situationally, and on the other hand, putting it in writing creates commitment. And, the biggest advantage, you can visualize your constitution every morning. In the morning, because it then activates your values for the day, and daily, so that this does not just happen on particular holidays (and thus has zero effect), but becomes a firm basis for your daily actions. We are truly the sum of our daily decisions, even the very small and seemingly banal and supposedly harmless, they add up and become automatisms that are difficult to discard, especially when practiced in the long run they harm us, it is particularly detrimental. This happens very often when negative emotions are making the decisions (rather than merely indicating that something needs our attention and mental resolution). Hanson refers to his therapy practice experience to make this clear: "Through much effort and the application of certain tricks, we may succeed in improving the momentary state of mind of others, making them feel comfortable. However, we usually do not take the time to consciously nurture and maintain this feeling so that it can *anchor itself in* the brain. I am also talking about myself here. As a therapist, it is a disappointing experience that of all the positive thoughts and feelings I strive to evoke in others, very little is of lasting value. [...] It doesn't matter whether one is in an executive education seminar or an Alcoholics Anonymous meeting. One always strives to set a positive process in motion - something that strengthens one's back, that makes one wiser, etc. - and yet often has to realize just a few hours later that any positive effect seems to have evaporated. Sisyphus sends his regards. As if the boulder we have so laboriously pushed up the slope always rolls back down by itself. The negative distortion is not our fault. But we can do something about it."[55]

The first step is not to wait until you can do something without fear according to your constitution (that will never happen). Do it with fear, when your heart beats up to your neck, you start shaking with stress and tension, you break out in a sweat - never mind - in the name of God, do it, the confidence and self-efficacy comes only with action, when you really stay true to yourself and respect yourself. It can also strengthen you in other ways. And that's what we're going to look at now.

NEGATIVE EMOTIONS VS. RESPONSIVE MODE

In Chapter "Emotions", I showed what happens and what it costs us to be in reactive "red" mode. Unfortunately, "the brain is like Velcro for negative experiences and like Teflon for positive ones. While the negativity bias ensures our survival in moments of existential threat, it impairs our quality of life, interpersonal relationships, personal development, and lasting health. [...] It is the default setting of the Stone Age brain. If we do not learn to master it, it will continue to dominate us. By learning to consciously embrace the good, we level the playing field and counteract the tendencies of negativity bias: We weaken negative thoughts, feelings, and actions, and strengthen positive. This exercise meets your three basic needs for security, satisfaction, and belonging."[56]

And here we find our two functional modes on the neuronal level:

"Every operating system of your brain knows two basic modes: an *adaptive* and a *reactive one*. As long as you feel that one of your basic needs is being met, the system in question is in adaptive mode. When you feel safe, your avoidance system operates in adaptive mode, giving you a feeling of relaxation and inner peace. When you feel satisfied, your reward system also switches to adaptive mode, giving you grateful and satisfied moments. And when you feel integrated and included, your attachment system operates in adaptive mode, evoking feelings of belonging, familiarity, and empathy. For the sake of simplicity, I would like to assign the color *green to* this mode.

In adaptive mode, you can meet challenges without letting them put you under pressure. It's as if your brain has a kind of shock absorber that prevents external events from shaking you up too much. You can cope even with power-sapping or threatening events without becoming frightened or frustrated. You are firmly rooted in life and able to cope with even difficult situations because you are never deprived of a basic feeling of security and safety.[57]

Since negative emotions cost us a lot and prevent us from feeling the positive ones, it is important to take care of the negative emotions first (especially when they are particularly present). I.e. to deal with them consciously and to ask them: "with what concern do you come to me?" and then to switch on the action-oriented thinking in order to ask oneself: "what can/will/should I sensibly do with it? " Here is the big trap of rumination waiting for you if you fail to leave emotional thinking, which leads to no solutions. How to properly work with and understand your emotions, and what techniques are useful for this, I have described in detail in my first book. Now let's look at what to do if you have actually understood your difficult emotions and also have solution strategies ready, but your emotions don't want to give you a break, because: "The mixture of brooding and bad mood is poison. Scientific evidence shows that people who brood in a sad and despairing mood are pessimistic and self-critical, feel at the mercy of others and powerless, and generally see everything in the black."[58] A negative downward spiral is created, which then becomes a self-fulfilling prophecy. "The evidence for the negative effects of rumination is overwhelming. If you think too much, you absolutely must get rid of this habit in order to become happier. In fact, I would argue that for brooders, one of the secrets to happiness is to stop obsessive ruminating and turn negative thoughts into neutral and positive ones. Truly happy people are able to immerse themselves in activities that divert their energies and attention from dark and anxiety-filled thoughts. [...] Becoming happier means learning to turn off your musings about minor and major negative experiences, to stop thinking about every if and why, and to not allow them to distort your image of yourself and the world."[59] That's why it's important to imperatively stop doing that, and first look for real solutions to your concerns in a neutral mood, or even better, a good mood. However, this should also not be too good, emotional extremes are to be avoided in decision-making.

Sonja Lyubomirsky suggests several strategies for this in her book:

1. Distraction, here e.g. yoga is also very helpful, but also everything else that occupies your mind with other content, but you should look for a fulfilling activity here, and not spam you away with your cell phone, for example.

2. Set aside fixed limited times to ponder: "so that's what I'm thinking about from 6:30-7:00 p.m."

3. Write down your thoughts (this also encourages thinking through to the end, plus sometimes you can see in black and white what a load of crap it is)

4. Talk to someone. Here's the rule: "But be careful. Choose your confidant carefully: He must be able to remain objective and not fall into brooding with you, because that will make [both of you] feel worse than before."[60] The person also must not shame you or downplay what you are telling. If you're unsure, it's better to just write down your thoughts. Talking to someone also helps, because in order to make someone understand what is going on inside you, you have to formulate your thoughts clearly - think them through to the end, (writing also serves this purpose) and, ideally, to get acceptance of the other person, who says: "you are allowed to feel this way."

5. The Stop Technique. "When you find yourself ruminating, think, say or shout "stop" or "no"."[61] This is, next to writing, my favorite technique: visualize a stop sign to break the chain of thoughts and ask yourself what you need for yourself, how you could do something good for yourself, what you are looking forward to today or if that doesn't want to succeed, then ask yourself what exactly you still have to do and picture how you want to tackle it very detailed step by step. The main thing is to silence the negative thoughts. Sometimes it helps to interrupt: "Oh no, you again" and occasionally a "Shut up" or a "Thank you, I'll take care of myself."

6. Since we are very situational, it is important to identify and avoid brooding traps: make a list of "typical places, times,

situations and people that make you brood. If at all possible, avoid these triggers or modify them so that you no longer fall into rumination. This is similar to giving up smoking: Smokers, too, must learn to avoid certain places, times of day, [situations] and people that make them crave a cigarette."[62]

7. If you're ruminating about something, it also helps to ask the "How important will this be a year from now or on your deathbed?" - question.

8. Learn to meditate. Meditation has very many beneficial effects; up to the lengthening of the telomeres. The most important thing with regard to brooding is: it helps to leave the thought pull that arises when brooding and also to learn to do this more and more quickly. It helps to take a certain distance to your own thinking and not to take every secretion of your brain at face value. It is also the method of choice if the methods described so far do not help and you have a major problem with compulsive brooding and anxiety, and these are already partly self-triggering.

Just see what works best for you. This does not mean: "I tried it once half-heartedly and it didn't help." If you've really tried the above methods and they don't do the trick, then we need to dig deeper; fortunately, "Unwinding Anxiety" by Judson A. Brewer has recently been published.[63] In it, he shows how you can unwind habitualized anxiety spirals that trigger automatic behavior, and can even be triggered by it themselves. Mindfulness and awareness (both abundant in meditation) are the tools of choice for this, as well as a basic understanding of how our brain works, i.e., how it learns and forms behavior and habits, and the criteria it uses to make choices. Only when we understand this and are able to actually manage it differently anything will change. As I pointed out at the beginning, there is a lot that makes it hard for us to change (see chapter "Take out the trash"). Ultimately, it all depends on our (handling of) emotions and the (previous) learning experiences of our brain, some of which we are not even consciously aware of as such. Things are just like that (part of our personality). That this is somehow not right, we only notice by the fact that we suffer.

Matthieu Ricard says so beautifully in his TED Talk about happiness, "Nobody wakes up in the morning and thinks to themselves: 'May I suffer all day today.' "

How is it that we do it anyway? We have already learned some reasons, they lie partly in our "socially" conditioned biology and in the functioning and the (early) learning experiences of our brain, which we are partly not aware of until we specifically analyze them (keyword beliefs). And the rest, unfortunately, we have taught ourselves, and we do not know that either. Only it permanently gets us down.

Here's Brewer's appearance: "Before you know it - because it's not really a conscious event - the way you deal with emotions or alleviate stressors becomes a habit. This is a defining moment, so please read this slowly: using the same brain mechanisms as [once caveman], we modern geniuses have gone *from learning to survive to* literally *killing* ourselves with these habits."[64]

How does this work? Simple, because our brains have been doing reward-based learning (operant conditioning) which is based on positive and negative reinforcement since time immemorial. "Simply put, you want to do more of the things that feel good (positive reinforcement) and less of the things that feel bad (negative reinforcement)."[65] Why this can be killer is explained by our emotions, if they are bad, the brain wants to get rid of them. Now, immediately, at any cost, the main thing is to do it quickly. Get rid of it now. And as we have seen, when we have big emotions and especially stress and fear, the prefrontal cortex is offline and thus unavailable, putting willpower and rational action out of reach. That's why you can't "think your way out" of such states and negative behaviors or master them with willpower. Thinking: "Smoking is bad for me, I should stop" alone has not yet led to any result.

Worse, the brain that is still available now is the one described above, and driven by emotion, it looks for a quick fix that it once learned. So we drink after hours to "get down", eat ice cream to "comfort" ourselves, stupidly scroll the cell phone to avoid thinking. The problem with Quick Fix is that on the one hand it is externally supplied; on the other hand it usually has very problematic consequences in the long run (if you always drink to relax you will develop an addiction problem in the long run) and it also does not bring a permanent solution. So you have to eat even more ice cream and drink even more alcohol, because the brain has also become accustomed to the "substance", and to achieve the same effect, it needs more and more of it.

Why do we do this if it's actually so bad? - Precisely because it has a short-term effect. We remember: "Get rid of it, quickly. NOW." is the slogan. The brain remembers, for example, that you are more relaxed and in a better mood when you drink. You drink. That's it. At some point, this happens almost automatically and hardly consciously, because your brain has made it a habit. The better you feel in the *short term* (the brain doesn't see the hangover, the excess weight, the self-loathing), the stronger the habit and the more automatic it becomes. If you get caught up in negative thoughts, and have the habit of ruminating, and then it degenerates into an uncontrolled endless downward spiral, it's a habit too, except that the trigger and quick fix here are your own negative thoughts. What's worthwhile about that? At the beginning, thinking through fears, problems and worries seems productive; after all, you're looking for a solution, playing it out in your mind - exactly - and feeling better for a short time as a result. But that doesn't last long and before you know it, it's a perpetual motion machine and you're no longer in the driver's seat, but completely at its mercy... At least that's how it feels.

Attention, here it is important: it is not about conceptual intellectual understanding of what I describe here, because we all "know" that already wonderfully, only it has not brought much. But it is about an immediate experience of what is happening right now in our environment, our body and in our thoughts. So let's write behind our ears: we can't think our way out of fear, we can't force our way out of it, not even with willpower and especially not with thoughts.

"I should/shouldn't do anything (or not do anything)." So what can we do?

Step 1

Recognize the habit loop: It consists of trigger, behavior, and outcome/reward.

Example:

Trigger: By hearing the name, the sight (through social media not really difficult), or thanks to the fact that my brain simply remembers; I remember a person who treated me badly. I feel tension in my body, tightness in my chest, how my shoulders pull up to my ears and how my heart beats faster, inner restlessness, the feeling of being at the mercy that I felt at that time comes up again, and the feeling of deep frustration to be in that situation.

Behavior: I imagine how I would have reacted better, what I would have done differently in the situation, and how I would have confronted the person and reprimanded him, and so on. I paint a really colorful picture and play it out again and again in many variations of how it "should" have gone. .... Over and over again.... And again ....and again...and again...and now in variation...but what if...but then....

Result, solution: in the short term I relax a little (relief), and I no longer feel so helpless and as a winner, since I have now solved the situation satisfactorily for me in my mind (reward) but the thoughts become more rather than less in the long run (habitualization, the brain gets used to and needs a higher dose for the desired effect). I start thinking through the same thing again....

Step 2: What do I get out of it in the short term (see above) and in the long term?

This costs me energy and exhausts me, poisons my mood, costs time and energy, and does not solve the problem, so the thoughts come again and again. The fear triggered by a thought attracts as a behavior further (negative) thoughts that fuel the spiral and trigger even more inner tension, stress and negative feelings.

Over the next 2 weeks, examine what anxiety habit loops you have, and what they are like: what are the triggers, what behavior you engage in (how you experience it and how it feels in the body is especially important here!), and what is the short-term result. Ask yourself also if possible during the process: what do I get out of it in the long run, how do I feel afterwards? Write down what you found out. Record your habit loops and whether the hoped-for "reward" is really that great in its long-term effect. It is more likely to be *disappointing*. That is why it is important that you feel (physically) these consequences of these habit spirals and your behavior as clearly as possible and that you experience and consciously perceive them as intensely as possible. Only in this way can your "stone age brain" learn that this is now no longer good! Only in such a way, and not differently. It cannot argue about it intellectually, it can only learn from real experience and contemplation that what it thought was good is not good, and instead something else must be found as a solution. The problem with our previous "solution" was, that it wasn't one. We wanted to "make our feelings go away quickly." To do this, we fed things from the outside (ice cream, alcohol, distraction) or from the inside (endless circling of thoughts, worrying, rumination); we had the urge to do something with the feeling to "make it go away."

Step 3: Ride the wave

Since "making it go away" doesn't work and only awakens mostly destructive desires that continue to drive the cycle, the question is: "what can one do with it in a meaningful way? " In principle, there is not much you can do, because we don't have much influence on many things, our thoughts come like waves, we also don't know what will happen in the future, and our influence on other people is rather rudimentary... So what to do with the waves of our mind? "You can't stop waves, you can only learn to surf them." - says Jon Kabat-Zinn. It means to curiously and mindfully observe the thoughts and let them pass by without having to "do something with them", but to accept them as they are, without resisting, because that is like pouring gasoline on the fire. It is not passivity, however, in which you are fully caught by the wave and swept away in the maelstrom of thoughts about your bad habits that sustain them. You watch with curiosity what exactly is happening in your body right now, what cravings are being awakened (if you have practiced steps 1 and 2, you can more easily withstand the impulse to follow them and just let them pass). You watch as the wave builds. You accept what is there and rest in the experience as it is right now until it dies down on its own because you don't add anything and find your way back to the beach on the back of the wave, where the wave ultimately arrives on its own....

When you manage to calmly allow thoughts to be without attaching to them, or trying to "fix" something, or suppressing them, space and freedom emerges to turn to them, observe them, and just let them go for what they are: byproducts of our brain which we genuinely give too much importance. Through deep breathing and relaxation exercises such as meditation, but also physical relaxation such as yoga or progressive muscle relaxation, you can very effectively support yourself in calming your firing amygdala. This is ultimately responsible for your sensations. You calm it more effectively by activating the parasympathetic nervous system with the aforementioned techniques than by rational arguments, because that part of the brain is in pause when the amygdala takes over.

And maybe now you can also see why the methods 1-7 mentioned at the beginning can only help with small things anyway, they are based on distraction and not on resolution. Please note that if you affirm positively, replace negative thoughts with positive ones, etc., that it is resistance; this also prevents resolution under certain circumstances. Resolution happens only through consciousness.

And so, once again, de Mello is right when he writes, "Awareness, awareness, and awareness again."[66] That's all it really takes.

RESPONSIVE MODE ENABLED

And then, fortunately, there are positive emotions that can be specifically sought out. "One who seeks the good does not deny or resist the bad. One is aware of the whole truth - of all the mosaic pieces of life - instead of seeing only the negative ones. One recognizes the good in oneself, in others, in the world, and in our common future."[67]

Since the good easily passes us by, and does not enter us as easily and deeply as negative emotions without our doing, certain steps are helpful to take in the good, which is *"theoretically speaking, the reflected internalization of positive experience into the implicit memory.*

This consists of four simple steps:

1. Have a positive experience.
2. Enrich it.
3. Take them into yourself.
4. Connect them with positive and negative material.

Step 1 activates a positive state of consciousness. Steps 2 to 4 install this in the brain. The first three steps focus entirely on dealing with positive experiences. The fourth step is optional, but very powerful: it makes use of positive thoughts and feelings to soothe, mitigate, and possibly replace negative ones."[68]

Since we are physical beings and perceive the world with our senses, there are "five factors that promote the conversion of fleeting mental experiences into permanent neuronal structures. The greater the *duration, intensity, multiplicity of modes, novelty, and personal relevance*, the more successful the storage in memory. Each of these factors holds the possibility of making neurons active so that synapses form more connections as you take in the good. Repeated episodes of taking in the good deepen the neural traces [and the more mass is created] [...] Forming new brain structures is basically a mechanical process."[69]

It's like going to the gym, just once a month is no use. To "re-polarize" the brain requires regular exercise, some mindfulness (to notice or bring to mind the opportunities, you can also remember or simply imagine things as part of such "exercise"), and the decision to engage with the experience (preferably with all your senses) and to follow the experience. If you notice a beautiful sunrise and just briefly think, "Oh nice, but now I have to do important adult things quickly and don't have time for that" then you are missing an opportunity. I think children have an advantage over us (as long as we haven't spoiled them): they can marvel at things big and small and spontaneously get completely involved, but with children it's completely unreflective. Think what you could do as an "adult" if only you let go of adult things... Let's stay with the sunrise: "Oh beautiful" You interrupt whatever you were doing and take the time to absorb the sight, marvel at the light, feel the warmth breaking through the coolness of the morning, (yes where exactly?) to breathe the fresh air, deeply and feel it fill your lungs, to hear the birds chirping - a free concert of joy at the new day beginning. "Every morning is world premiere" it is called, and you are lucky to be there and in the front row. You are taken by this beauty and feel wonder at how everything is interconnected and interdependent, and that you are a part of this universe and thus never alone. You feel a comforting warmth in your heart and a sense of connection and an all-encompassing compassion for all of creation, you want all creatures to be well and to protect the world because it is such a wonderful place.

Not bad for a crummy sunrise, right?[70] Along the way, a switch from hedonistic to eudaimonic happiness takes place here. That brings us to the next topic:

WHAT IS HAPPINESS?

It is not the external things, as I wrote at the beginning, even if we want to believe it so much. Even money is ineffective above a certain level of income, two years after marriage you have the same level of happiness as before (and if you are unlucky a lower one), the total of external factors accounts for only 10% of happiness, says Lubomirsky in her book.[71] Thanks to hedonistic adaptation, we also quickly get used to them, which further lowers their happiness potential and new external things must be strived for.

50% are probably in the genes, these determine our "fixed point of happiness" to which we return again and again after tragedies or triumphs.

The remaining 40 % is work. Because "happiness is work" [...] It is probably self-evident that every great achievement in life - such as learning a profession, mastering a sport or raising a child - also requires great effort. Nevertheless, we often find it difficult to apply this insight to our emotional and spiritual lives. [72]

This includes a certain amount of expertise so that you don't seek happiness in the wrong place or in the wrong way, such as was the case with the "I'm-so-happy-if-I-just-talk-about-it-often-enough" affirmation hype that is now known as "toxic optimism." You need a basic knowledge of how things work to apply them effectively, and of course you need to apply them to make them work.

Let's start with some trivia that is not so trivial: if you want to be miserable with a guarantee of success, here is a simple recipe: don't sleep 6 hours (preferably after drinking alcohol, so you don't get into deep sleep), hastily eat sugary industrially processed junk as you pass by, which robs you of the last of your energy, and start fights because you're tired and overstimulated, and generally hate people because they're exhausting, and constantly want something from you... et voilà.

Wasn't so hard, was it? If you have a lot of bad habits, then it really was quite easy... and you'll have a lot of work ahead of you to be happy. But it's worth it: "When we are happier, we not only experience more joy, contentment, love, pride, and wonder, we improve other aspects of our lives such as our energy, our immune system, our engagement at work, our relationships with others, and our physical and mental health. When we become happier, we also increase our self-confidence and self-esteem. And it's not just ourselves who benefit when we become happier people, but also our partners, families, friends, acquaintances and society as a whole."[73]
Happiness is more the sum of the everyday choices and behaviors you make in your life, less an ecstatic state.

So what do you do every day? I hope for your sake you don't have an addiction problem, or engage in behavior that is reprehensible by moral (and/or legal) standards. Then there will be no happiness, because an essential ingredient is to be a decent person, and free in your choices. If you are addicted to something, you are not free. That is the necessary condition. Otherwise, it's like trying to drive off in a car without wheels: it doesn't matter how great the rest of the car is, you can't really get going, and if by some miracle you roll a few meters, the crash inevitably comes.

So if the above is not a topic, let's start with the then most important: sleep, because without sleep everything is stupid. Regular restful sleep of 7-9 hours is important; the body can recover and regenerate, in certain sleep phases cleaning processes in the brain take place. Sufficient and regular sleep also promotes regular meals, whereas lack of sleep leads to weight gain, as the hormone ghrelin is increased (appetite stimulation) and thus the feeling of hunger especially for unhealthy sugary or fatty stuff, as the overtired body demands energy. Erin Hanlon, a Chicago endocrinologist puts it this way: "Under sleep deprivation, the craving for even certain comforting foods becomes stronger and the ability to resist them is apparently weakened. Thus, one automatically eats more." It is advisable to always keep roughly the same bedtimes (even on weekends), to sleep in a rather cool, dark and quiet room, and to avoid screens and exciting news. Thanks to chapter "Negative emotions vs. responsive mode", you won't be tossing worrying thoughts around at night ;)

Next comes the food: Food not only provides energy, it also serves to renew and build the body's cells.

Accordingly, it is obvious to avoid industrially processed foods, they are simply nutritionally worthless, full of sugar and stabilizers and flavor enhancers are and still heavily oversalted and low in fiber (and it really does not matter what is written on the package, even if it is "vegan"). For these reasons, you should not choose any "light" products, because the flavor carrier fat is simply replaced by sugar in the unhealthiest variations, e.g. by industrially produced fructose, which is true poison.
The natural fructose is packed just right, in fruit with a lot of fiber, of which one does not eat huge amounts, on the other hand, already in fruit juice the ratio is unfavorable, therefore juices should be avoided. From 25g per meal, natural fructose is problematic for everyone; it is also the most common intolerance. In case of suspected intolerances, it is best to have the hydrogen breath test for fructose malabsorption and lactose intolerance first.

Industrially produced fructose from corn starch is added to foods in unprecedented doses. Fructose has a significantly higher sweetening power than glucose. By reducing the glucose content while increasing the fructose content, the sweetening power of a syrup can be significantly increased without changing the substance content. Therefore, increasing the fructose content by converting the glucose is economical, since a comparable sweetening power is achieved with a smaller amount of material - from which you can see how much the manufacturer cares about your well-being...

The problem: Products sweetened with High Fructose Corn Syrup (HFCS) do not produce a feeling of satiety in the body - quite different from what happens after eating simple glucose (dextrose). There is evidence that fructose is preferentially stored as fat, especially in the form of liver fat and visceral abdominal fat. Too much fructose ingested can basically no longer be converted into glucose after a certain point. Fructose is then alternatively metabolized in the liver to fatty acids and in this way can promote the accumulation of body fat. Unlike glucose, fructose is metabolized largely independently of insulin. Since insulin indirectly plays a role in generating the feeling of satiety and, moreover, fructose in higher amounts is thought to promote fat synthesis, the heavy use of HFCS as a sweetener can lead to obesity, metabolic syndrome, high blood pressure, gout or even chronic kidney damage, as well as non-alcoholic fatty liver. And this already in children! A close connection between the increased consumption of fructose (especially in the form of HFCS) and the occurrence of obesity, lipometabolic disorders, high blood pressure, elevated uric acid levels and a diabetic metabolic condition is assured. Depression may also follow due to tryptophan deficiency.

To do something good for yourself, you should avoid sweets and sugar, as well as alcohol as far as possible.

In order to do something good not only for yourself, you should drastically limit the consumption of meat, and if you choose meat, then choose organic meat. It is really unbearable what we do to the animals before we eat them.[74] It's not healthy for us either. Not for anything or anyone, and not for the planet. As you can see, there is a lot going on on your plate. Because it votes three times a day on what kind of world you want to live in, how the creatures in it are doing, and also what your body should consist of.

Before you now declare your body the most sacred temple that deserves only exquisite superfood, let me tell you, there is no superfood. But there are fresh seasonal and regional products, high-quality vegetable fats, many different vegetables and fruits, and if you want meat / fish in small quantities and not from factory farming / aquaculture, and plenty to drink (water, green tea, herbal tea) best 2-3 liters a day. If you eat a varied, colorful, plant-based diet, and prepare your food fresh, then that's great. This is then also enough.

If you are a "healthy eating" newbie, the following tips may help you avoid certain mistakes when starting out, which are:
- I quickly eat what is there (just throw it away)
- and I start on Monday/ next month etc.
Get started right away.

It is a mistake to let it be in 100%, because you think it too complicated and thereby think you can not start. Start directly with a first change. For example, leave out soft drinks or sweets or processed foods. Part of this, especially at the beginning, is not wanting to change too much at once. Ask yourself, "what will I benefit most from?" e.g. "don't drink soda anymore," and start there, then plan further steps and their implementation afterwards. Because in the long run, you really won't get far without a very specific plan.

Create a weekly menu plan, e.g. always at rest on Sundays, because the situation "there is nothing to eat" and "I do not know what (healthy) to eat " should thus be avoided. Plan shopping and food preparation times with the expected course of the coming week in mind. If you know you're in for a long, stressful day with an uncertain outcome, the magic word is Meal Prep. If you come home completely wrecked late at night, you won't start peeling the veggies....

Preparation is done with food scales, it's a bit laborious at first, but the point is to get a feel for portion sizes. Over time, you'll know them and have the recipes down quickly if you combine that with using a food tracking app. Food tracking takes place BEFORE you eat: to raise awareness of nutritional content and modify your planned meal if necessary, and also to achieve a conscious engagement with food. You don't do this until doomsday either, but for about 3 months to actually see clearly what you are eating, when and how, and to get a good feel for food portions. Most people completely underestimate the amounts they eat and like to forget about their snacks.

A few more pointers: you should never eat hastily while standing or walking around have a seat – hereby chew calmly, consciously and slowly, otherwise your body won't register it as proper food intake, and you'll tend to eat more - and it's no fun gobbling your food like a pelican, either, at least as long as you're not a pelican.

For the metabolism, 4-5 hour breaks between meals are a blessing, you should not skip breakfast, rather practice dinner cancelling.

If something unhealthy comes your way: please don't have an "it doesn't matter now" attitude and push another avalanche of food sins after it. It happened and move on. Just because you ate junk at lunch, it doesn't preclude a good salad in the evening. But: avoid strict bans. Plan for "treats" occasionally and then eat them with gusto.

It's not about never eating a piece of cake again, but about establishing the habit of eating consciously and healthily in general, and enjoying food.

Case even more important than food in your life is the question "with whom?" We are social beings, and dealing with people is an essential part of our lives. The people in it should be chosen wisely (I hinted at this in chapter Radical Action), because they generally have a lot of influence on us. People who drag you down or bring out the bad in you, and who do not respect your boundaries, should be rigorously removed from your life and you should seek out other people. This may sound very harsh to some ears at first, but we are very situational and impressionable[75] , and if you surround yourself with people with problems, they will soon become yours. Don't play the heroic savior either, many people don't want to be saved, they just want someone else to carry their problems for them. Don't think you are as smart as Odysseus to get away scot-free from the sirens. If Odysseus had been smart, he wouldn't have sailed there in the first place.

Look for people who will help you grow. Who are there for you without taking responsibility for you. People who will comfort you in defeats, but also celebrate your victories with you without envy. People who can have a lot of fun with you, but who will also take you aside and admonish you honestly when you do something incredibly stupid. People who may have goals like you do, or with whom you can share a commitment to something. People who honestly care about your well-being. Be such a person yourself.

Remember: You can't change the people around you, but you can change the people around you....

Another lucky charm is exercise. Move, preferably in nature, but in general, the sport you choose should be really fun. Sports help to burn calories (ideal would be 1000 - 1500 from exercise at least 3-4 times a week). Since we humans are built to be very energy efficient, sports do not work wonders calorically, but they do build muscle mass, which burns more calories than fat when at rest, plus sports improve body composition and body image. From a health point of view, moderate sport (here, too, the dose makes the poison) reduces high blood pressure and keeps the vessels elastic, strengthens the heart, improves fitness and the immune system. In addition, sport also promotes mental well-being by reducing stress, and depending on the type of sport also brings sociability, and ideally you do it in nature, which in itself is very beneficial.

Especially beginners should rather do something every day to "keep at it", even if it is "only" 15 minutes at the beginning, but really every day - and at the same time. This saves you from thinking about if, when and if at all, haggling over exceptions and excuses why not today. Think about a pool of activities and choose from it flexibly according to your mood. E.g. you don't always feel like running or strength training, then it can also be a yoga session. Whatever you do, it is best to insert the exercise session between two already established habits, e.g. between getting up and showering. Doing something for yourself in the morning also strengthens your sense of self-efficacy, and exercise in particular gets your circulation going for the day better than any coffee could.

And very importantly, "for many people, physical activity is a key habit that triggers broader changes. "Exercise radiates to other areas," says James Prochaska, a researcher at the University of Rode Island. "It somehow promotes the formation of other, positive habits."[76]

HABITS

You have probably already noticed: what you do all day is largely controlled by automatic habits. Rainer Tschechne writes: „Every habit will always serve two purposes. It will fit in with the people who live with us, and at the same time it will sustain our life in this environment and satisfy our most important needs. Habits must therefore: 1. ensure for the environment that it is not disturbed in its functioning, and 2. satisfy basic needs, that is, maintain life, eat, drink, sleep, achieve protection from disease and injury, etc. First of all, our habits ensure that we fit into our family. This family is unlikely to align itself with what would be most promising for our future.[77] Many of the habits that were programmed into me corresponded to the interests and structure of the environment in which I found myself, and throughout life they try to ensure my functioning by their continued existence. Each of us must draw the conclusion from this: The purpose of my habits is not at all my individual advancement. They are primarily to ensure that I fit as well as possible into the environment into which I was born. In addition, there is another disadvantage: because I was born into something that had existed without me for a long time, I had no chance to actively shape the rules I had to follow myself."[78] Unfortunately, I still have full responsibility for it. And there's another problem: "My habits make the past the future. "[79] You reproduce the same damaging behaviors, feelings, relationship structures, etc. via your habits until you reach your usual "happiness level." Tschechne speaks here of decades of experience as a therapist: "If I want to predict how a person from my environment will behave tomorrow, I now achieve a high hit rate. The more precisely I know how he behaved yesterday, the higher the hit rate. The assumption: A person does not change. He will behave in the future as he has behaved in the past is very often true. This does not mean that people cannot change. Only, the rule is - unfortunately or thank God - that they do not. [...] You may have noticed that I said above: Most people behave tomorrow as they behaved yesterday. I did not say: they behave as they wanted to behave yesterday. Nor did I say: they want to behave the way they behaved yesterday."[80]

The reason for this is the deeply ingrained habits within us: "The program that has once established itself as a habit rules. The habit stands against reason, insight and will. Anything we do to consciously and planned change in our behavior encounters natural hurdles that make it difficult to implement. Therefore, give yourself extenuating circumstances if you want to optimize your habits. Your nature opposes the plan. Your need for security, which wants to hold on to everything that has been stable until now; your basic needs and instincts, which follow a millennia-old program; and your biological construction, which sets insurmountable limits to self-control and brain power: these are its foundations, and there is no point in ignoring them."[81]

Therefore, it is not surprising that the best remedy against habit is habit. The only thing that helps against habit is habit, because it takes the place of the one you have unconsciously established, which may be contributing to your current unhappiness. A habit loop consists of a trigger stimulus, a routine (behavior), and a reward. This is a basic learning process. The habit is formed only [when a desire is felt, when the trigger stimulus is merely seen or otherwise perceived]. [...] New habits are formed by putting together a trigger stimulus, a routine, and a reward, and then reinforcing a craving that drives the loop. Take smoking, for example. When a smoker sees a trigger stimulus - say a pack of Marlboro - for example, his brain anticipates a nicotine rush. Even the sight of cigarettes is enough to make the brain crave a nicotine rush. If this does not occur, the craving increases until the smoker, involuntarily, reaches for a cigarette. [...] *This explains why habits are so powerful: They create a neuronally anchored craving.* [...] Particularly strong habits generate addictive responses, so that "desires become compulsive cravings," forcing our brains into autopilot, "even in the face of strong negative incentives such as loss of reputation, job, home, and family.""[82]

The good news, you can change habits (though not eliminate them). "The rule is that if you use the same trigger stimulus and give the same reward, you can change the routine and change the habit. [...] The trigger stimulus must create not only a routine but also a desire for the future reward."[83]

The procedure to change habit loops consists of the following steps:

- Identify the routine
- Experiment with rewards
- Isolate the trigger (usually location, time, emotional state, other people, immediately preceding action).
- Establish a plan: Implementation Intentions = Formulate implementation intentions in advance, along the lines of "if x, then I will do yz."[84]

A little warning, or rather a hint to behavior change. Duhigg writes: "Researchers began to find that replacing habits works quite well for many people until severe psychological distress [...] occurs. Then alcoholics often reach for the bottle again. Researchers asked why habit replacement, if it is otherwise so effective, fails at such critical moments. [...] they found that replacement habits only become lasting new behaviors when they are accompanied by something else. [...] [That element was faith.] Even teaching people better habits doesn't eliminate the reason they started drinking in the first place. At some point they'll have a bad day, and no new routine will make everything seem okay. That's where believing in that you can manage stress without alcohol can make a difference."[85] In my opinion, this requires not only a change in behavior, but a change in self-image that perceives oneself as self-efficient in achieving one's goals and adhering to one's values. This doesn't happen overnight, and is especially shaken during emotionally difficult times (regressing from extreme stress into early, more firmly established behaviors that are then "more retrievable") when the amygdala takes over.

What can also benefit you is increased willpower (or: self-control, perseverance), as it affects all areas of life. The Stanford University marshmallow experiment should have gotten around, it shows that ultimately it's about the ability to defer gratification, and that it's a skill that can be learned: "The children who were able to ignore the marshmallows apparently possessed self-regulatory skills that benefited them throughout their lives."[86] Willpower is trainable on small things, e.g., making the bed, performing small tasks conscientiously, such as setting the table, getting up immediately at the first alarm bell, etc.

It can be trained like a muscle, but also exhausts itself when used during the day, which is why diets usually fail in the evening and people also like to argue with their partner after work.

This is because willpower is fed from one tank for everything, and this tank is emptied by:

- Stress
- Decisions
- Emotional control
- Self-control
- Fatigue
- Hunger
- Being a recipient of orders instead of acting in a self-determined manner

If there wasn't much in it to begin with, the tank will quickly run dry. You can strengthen your willpower by training and using it with foresight. Only if you fill the tank is there anything in it. If you just pull the fuel gauge with your finger, it won't do any good.

You have taught yourself through inconsistency not to take yourself seriously; it's time to reverse that. The feeling of your own self-efficacy (which is closely coupled with genuine self-worth) - takes a hit; you think you're incapable if you keep taking on things only to abandon them altogether. A feeling of self-efficacy only arises when you can anticipate that your projects, which you turn to and for which you are responsible, will actually succeed most of the time (from experience). Setbacks and missteps inevitably come, but failure is to leave it altogether. It will never be perfect, we are not robots.

Important to strengthen your willpower: make many decisions once, according to the scheme if situation x, then I do y, to relieve yourself and have a guide ready, especially for difficult situations. Or if you decide to do sports every day, you don't have to decide every day anew and fight with yourself if and when and if at all.

It is important to make habits out of the new behaviors that no longer require thinking and willpower, this relieves the willpower too. As humans, we are very situational and nowadays not (anymore) in a neutral environment, but in one that constantly tries to influence us (keyword smartphone). Willpower alone is not enough to survive, certainly not if it is not well trained.

Hordes of psychologists, engineers, chemists, programmers are working on the fact that you cannot let go of the slot machine (keyword smartphone also fits here), on the bliss point (50% carbohydrates 35% fat & salt = chips), on your shopping behavior and how it can be influenced... An entire industry creates products that we can't let go of and that are unhealthy, catches us with our pants down on the toilet to push a product on us in a weak moment, and incessantly records our psychological profile to be able to manipulate us even better, and never gets tired of it. But you do. So: manipulate your environment and external influencing factors in your favor and think about strategies in advance that protect your interests. And remember "don't sail that way" is wise, because willpower is finite.

Let's make an example, suppose you don't want to shovel candy into yourself indiscriminately anymore. Do everything you can to try out what helps you best to leave it alone:

- not have in stock
- don't start eating (it's easier to give up the first bite than the rest, because the (stone age) brain remembers "hey that's sweet, give it to me, who knows if there will be anything later")
- Divert attention for 20 minutes, the brain "forgets" the subject afterwards
- Have alternatives ready for snacking and tell yourself "if it's really hunger, I'll eat this apple"
- with sweet stuff, the brain thinks of immediate reward and awakens the desire for it. Colorfully imagine the long-term negative health consequences, and also how angry you will be with yourself after eating all that crap. It makes the supposed reward less attractive.
- Consider alternative actions in advance that you can apply directly to the key stimulus: e.g. instead of eating out of frustration, I call a friend, do a short meditation, play with my dog, etc.
- Here, of course, you observe your snacking habit loop and identify the actual emotional needs behind it that you can satisfy differently, if necessary.

See what works best for you and stick with it. And snack now and then with pleasure and joy, we are not robots after all. But then eat because you really want to eat it, that's the difference ;)

AD REM

We are getting to the point now? Admittedly, because it doesn't work without some basic insights. We have a false understanding of ourselves, which always flatters us, but is of no use. Quite the opposite. "If you look at economic textbooks, you will read that this homo economicus thinks like Albert Einstein, stores information like IBM's supercomputer *Big Blue* and has a willpower like Mahatma Ghandi. The people we know, of course, are not like that. Real people have trouble with division without calculators, sometimes forget their spouse's birthday, and have hangovers on New Year's morning."[87] In our own minds, it's no different. We think of ourselves (unquestioningly) as super, and everyone else as stupid, and believe we know exactly what we are doing and why, and why it is right and moral. To say the least, we have no idea how we were formed, and what really drives us and what constraints we are subject to. We have no idea that we consider ourselves a priori and unfoundedly (!) more moral and better than the others. At the same time, we have no idea how our own brain works and what it is doing to us right now, and what basic demands are made on us as a result. We consider our thoughts to be true and right, while they are so often puny and simply wrong, and yet they determine our lives. There is this beautiful saying, which cannot be clearly attributed to a source, which sums it up:

"Watch your thoughts, for they become words; watch your words, for they become actions; watch your actions, for they become habits; watch your habits, for they become your character; watch your character, for it becomes your destiny."

But because we think we know, we never really get embarrassed to see what is. To see clearly what is you need expertise, real insight that usually comes with humility, the willingness to deal with painful things and the will to actively shape things in your life. Permanent. This is not a 14 day quick fix program, you are experiencing fundamental changes deep within you that you need to establish and nurture... at least until they become habit. You also need to accept basic truths, such as that basic needs are called that because they are, and if you ignore them, you will fall flat on your face. That's why in a book on peace of mind you'll also find advice on sleep, food and exercise, because that's integral. We are physical beings, and everything is interwoven and affects each other.

Extremely helpful in seeing clearly, also in recognizing how interwoven everything is, is meditation. Best known is Jon Kabat-Zinn's definition of meditation: "Mindfulness involves being attentive in a certain way: consciously, in the present moment, and without judgment." You observe "what it is thinking inside you" without attaching to it, without having to do anything with it, and without becoming absorbed by it. You watch yourself thinking and realize that thoughts are merely constructs of your mind to which you attach meaning, this then causing a certain effect. You are aware without doing anything, only as an observer, which helps you to gain distance from your own thoughts and not to be taken over by them. You learn to accept things as you are and thus to be calm.

Research labs have shown that even relatively short-term meditation on untrained subjects produces measurable changes in the brain, with meditation-trained monks rocking this event: " During meditation on compassion [also known as Loving Kindness or metta meditation], most experienced meditators showed a dramatic increase in high-frequency brain activity, or gamma waves, "in a way that has never been described before in the neuroscience literature," reports Richard Davidson. [...] "We have found that the trained mind or brain is *physically different from* an untrained one. It won't be long before we understand the potential importance of mind training and thereby increase the likelihood that it will be taken seriously."[88] Ricard writes:

"'Ten thousand hours may sound daunting and may seem entirely unattainable to most of us, but there is comforting news. A study published by Richard Davidson, Jon Kabat-Zinn and others has shown that over the course of three months of meditation training, busy employees of a biotechnology company in Madison saw their frontal lobe activity shift significantly from right to left. [=which simply means they became happier] the immune system of these "meditation apprentices" was also strengthened.[89] Meditation has a health-promoting effect on the entire body, not only by improving the brain's resilience to stress, but also by positively stimulating the vagus nerve (rest and relaxation nerve), which in turn triggers positive health effects on a physical level. According to some studies, meditation even affects the length of telomeres, i.e. it has an effect down to the cellular level, and in that case it is rejuvenating. If you like, meditation is the original source of responsive mode.

I hope you have already played a little bit with the conscious experience of the responsive mode with the instructions from chapter Responsive Mode enabled. The good and positive feelings will occupy us now predominantly.

And here, too, meditation plays a major role. Barbara Fredrickson, in her research under the "broaden-and-build" theory[90] , was able to show that just 80-90 minutes of metta meditation a week has an extremely beneficial effect on positive feeling, which in turn "give[s] us the opportunity to enter a new level of our being: to broaden our minds (broaden) and build ourselves a new future (build). [...] The latest science shows that our daily emotional experiences influence the course of our lives [and our health, brain, and even genome]."[91]
The more joy, gratitude, cheerfulness, interest, hope, pride, pleasure and love (we'll look at those separately later) you experience in relation to your negative emotions, the more open you are, your consciousness expands, you are more creative, but also more helpful and full of compassion. Fredrickson says: "A positive outlook on life makes us better people. By opening our hearts and minds, we can discover, explore, and build new skills, new bonds, new knowledge, and new possibilities of our being."[92]

For the ratio of negative to positive feelings (although Fredrickson also says that the negative ones naturally weigh more heavily) she has determined a quotient together with Marcial Losada. She calls it the positivity ratio.[93] If the ratio is 1:1 or below, then a depression is to be assumed, with 2:1 one slouches around in life - these two groups unite unfortunately approx. 80% of the test results. Only at a quotient of 3:1 does the growing and blossoming begin, and the difference is not gradual. Rather, as she says: "like between water and ice." The positive feelings set in motion an upward spiral at a certain "dose" that allows for a diametrically different life. Here, too, we have a dichotomy that already runs through the entire book as a common thread. And there is another common thread: "In fact, current research has shown that permanently changing one's positive quotient requires as much determination, effort, and a change in one's lifestyle as dieting or lowering one's cholersterol levels." [94]

So here too it is: ex nihilo nihil, and since without love everything is nothing, let us now consider love. 2.0. "New science illuminates for the first time how love and its absence fundamentally alters the biochemicals by which your body is imbued. The love you experience or don't experience today can literally change important aspects of your cellular architecture next season and next year - cells that affect your physical health, vitality and overall well-being. In this way and beyond, just as your supply of clean air and nutritious food predicts how long you will walk this earth - and whether you will thrive or just get by - so does your supply of love. "[95]

For Fredrickson, love is not limited to sexual desire, kinship, or the chosen special bond with a single love partner: "If you limit your view of love to relationships or close bonds, love becomes a complex and confusing thicket of emotions, expectations, and insecurities. But when you focus your gaze on your body's definition of love, a clear path emerges to guide you through this thicket and lead you to a better life. [...] I must ask you to also let go of some of your most cherished beliefs about love: the idea that love is exclusive, permanent, and unconditional. These deeply held beliefs are often more wish than reality in people's lives. [...] Love, as you will see, is not permanent. It is, in fact, much more fleeting than most of us would like to admit. On the other hand, however, love is always renewable. And perhaps even more difficult to accept is that it is not unconditional. It doesn't show up no matter what, regardless of the conditions. On the contrary, you will see that the love your body craves is extremely sensitive to contextual cues. Love follows certain conditions. However, once you understand these conditions, you can find love countless times every day. "

According to Fredrickson, love is: "a momentary rise of closely interwoven events: first, the sharing of one or more positive emotions between you and another; second, a synchronicity between your biochemistry and behavior and that of the other person; and third, a reflected motive to invest in the other's well-being that produces mutual caring. My acronym for this trio is positivity resonance." [96]

These are only fleeting micro-moments, but their impact on us, if they occur correspondingly frequently and regularly, is of great and transforming power. This understanding of love, which is based on certain (also physical) conditions and a conscious and open engagement in the connection with the other person, also explains very well why some marriages are mere empty shells, while you can feel real closeness and deep connection with a stranger. This kind of connection sometimes arises spontaneously, but as has already been said, it is conditional - one of which conditions is security. If you do not feel security, feeling love is not possible. If you are not physically present (at most it is still possible in video or telephone conversations in real time) and also emotionally absent, you will not be able to establish any significant connection.

Thus Fredrickson correctly concludes, "this new view tells us with some urgency, [love] is something we should recultivate every morning, every afternoon, and every evening. Seeing love as positivity resonance motivates us to hug more often or share an inspiring or silly idea or picture over breakfast [with our partner]. [To be in true connection.] In this small way, we plant additional seeds of love that help our bodies; our well-being and our marriage grow stronger. "[97]

And then add to that countless moments in your day where you can make that connection with all people (and I'm almost inclined to say, and animals too).

A quote from Virginia Satir comes to mind in this context: "We need four hugs a day to survive. We need eight hugs a day to take care of ourselves. We need twelve hugs a day to grow up." She intuited that we need genuine connection and loving closeness to bring our full potential to fruition and blossom, and then to share it with others as "real" adults. This makes us better people and is good for others.

I love it when all the threads come together : D

SLEEP, EAT, MEDITATE, LOVE, REPEAT

So as we can see, "positive" emotions are really badass, and having many and good ones on a daily basis is very very desirable. In this book you found many hints and current research results on how to do this and what factors are necessary to be able to awaken and experience positive emotions authentically and thereby also grow as a person.

Take good care of yourself, physically and mentally. Pay attention to your sleep, your diet and your habits. Check your behavior to see if it really corresponds to the good image you have of yourself. Meditate. Be open, grateful for everything you have and don't be stingy with affection, seek the closeness of positive and constructive people and commit yourself to something bigger than yourself.

Go out into nature. Pause. Listen. Simply perceive. Take a deep breath. Imagine how every living thing, every human being, every animal, every plant on this planet is breathing at the same time as you are, how you are connected in breath to all living beings. We are part of a great whole. The best way to get in touch with this truth is in nature, where everything is interwoven and interdependent. We all want to live and be happy and avoid suffering. Everyone can contribute to this, including you. I wish you much joy in doing so.

TABLE OF CONTENTS

BIBLIOGRAPHY AND REFERENCES

Note on quotations: my insertions /changes or omissions [...] are always marked by square brackets. Emphases in the text are those of the authors, or marked as "by me" - if different. Spelling has been modernized where appropriate. All translations into German are by me. Internet pages show the date of the most recent call. I can warmly recommend the purchase of the titles mentioned here.

---

[1] De Mello, Anthony, " Der Springende Punkt. Wach werden und glücklich sein." Herder, Neuausgabe 2011. p. 93
(Original title, which doesn't sound like a fortune cookie, is Awareness, by the way. And more accurate.)

[2] Roth, Gerhard: entsteht Persönlichkeit? In Tagesspiegel: https://www.tagesspiegel.de/wissen/was-kinder-praegt-fruehkindliche-einfluesse-hinterlassen-spuren-im-gehirn/11876126-2.html accessed on 2020-03-22 (Fascinating in the context is also the research in the field of epigenetics).

[3] Ibid.

[4] Jahn, Izabela Luiza: Von Gestörten muss man sich fernhalten. BOD 2019. p .112 English Edition: "Stay away from idiots."

[5] In my book mentioned above, I go into all these phenomena in great detail. Among other things, it also deals with how a diametrically different life can be led through certain conscious decisions and targeted changes in thinking and behavior. This is about the techniques of discarding repression, making beliefs visible and learning how to influence emotions, and how to handle toxic people, but also how to have happy relationships.
Psychology allows a certain level of self-knowledge, without which, in fact, everything is nothing. We live mechanically, trapped in unhealthy patterns of behavior, and do not know what is happening

to us. The book is aimed at all those who are stuck in unhappy relationships, or do not progress in their personal development, or always fail at the same point, or simply want to live their relationships better, for which self-knowledge is the instrument of choice. But it is not the last word. That's why you are reading this now.

[6] Peterson, Jordan: "Jordan Peterson on how to free your soul from the past W/Joe Rogan." https://youtu.be/U_tJTAgHiPo Translation into German by me. Page accessed on 2020-09-08
Excellent short video, I highly recommend watching it.

[7] Covey, Stephen R.: Die sieben Wege zur Effektivität. Ein Konzept zur Meisterung Ihres beruflichen und privaten Lebens. Campus. 1996. p.30-31 emphasis mine.

[8] Peterson, Jordan: "Jordan Peterson on how to free your soul from the past W/Joe Rogan." https://youtu.be/U_tJTAgHiPo Translation into German by me.

[9] Jahn, Izabela Luiza: Von Gestörten muss man sich fernhalten. BOD 2019 / English Edition 2022 „Stay away from idiots."

[10] Covey, Stephen R.: Die sieben Wege zur Effektivität. Ein Konzept zur Meisterung Ihres beruflichen und privaten Lebens. Campus. 1996. S.80

[11] Ibid p.69

[12] Ibid p.73

[13] Ibid p.76

[14] Frankl, Viktor

[15] David Schnarch: Die Psychologie sexueller Leidenschaft. Piper 2015.

[16] "Kto z kim przystaje takim sie staje."

[17] The best thing to do is to create a list of people whose opinions you seriously value because they have earned it, and disregard everyone else.

[18] See page 13 and in "Stay away from idiots"

[19] Warner Bros: Big Bang Theory, season 7 episode 1 "Drinks from Strangers" from minute 15.

[20] Brown, Brené: Verletzlichkeit macht stark. Wie wir unsere Schutzmechanismen aufgeben und innerlich reich werden. Goldmann. 2017. p.186

[21] Gottman, John: Die 7 Geheimnisse der glücklichen Ehe. Ullstein. 2012. p. 257

[22] Ibid p. 277-278 emphasis mine.

[23] Ibidem p. 226-227

[24] Ibidem p. 229

[25] Ibidem p. 223

[26] Grawe, Klaus: Neuropsychotherapie. Hofgrewe. 2004. p. 185f

[27] Hanson, Rick: Denken wie ein Buddha. Gelassenheit und innere Stärke durch Achtsamkeit. (Original title: Hardwiring Happiness). Heyne 2018. p. 23 emphasis by Hanson.

[28] Ibid. S. 28

[29] Ibid. S. 46

[30] Ibid. S. 39

[31] Ibid. S. 39

[32] Ibid. S. 43

[33] Ibid. S. 40

[34] Ibid. S. 45

[35] Ibid. p. 40 Hanson refers here to research results of Gottman and Fredrickson, which we will discuss in more detail in this book.

[36] Ibid. S. 41-42

[37] Brzezinski, Milosz: "#16 Zyciologia, czyli jak ogarniac poza praca. Milosz Brzeziniski cz.2." Podcast "Wysoko wydajni" by Michal Kowalczyk. https://youtu.be/bdGbDrZKenQ from minute 33. Page accessed on 20.12.2020

[38] Cloud, H.; Townsend, J.: "Nein sagen ohne Schuldgefühle. Gesunde Grenzen setzen." SCM Hänssler. 2017. S. 169

[39] There is a very nice article about restoring trust at WikiHow, I found it while researching the topic: https://de.wikihow.com/Vertrauen-wieder-aufbauen Page accessed on 22/01/2021

[40] Ibid

[41] Hanson, Rick: : Denken wie ein Buddha. Gelassenheit und innere Stärke durch Achtsamkeit. (Original title: Hardwiring Happiness). Heyne. 2018. pp. 65-66

[42] Ibid. S. 67-69

[43] Ibid. S. 69

[44] https://dgek.de/was-ist-emotionale-kompetenz/ Page accessed on 28.01.2021

[45] Ibid

[46] Covey, Stephen R.: Die sieben Wege zur Effektivität. Ein Konzept zur Meisterung Ihres beruflichen und privaten Lebens. Campus. 1996. p.92-93. emphasis mine.

[47] Ibidem p. 101

[48] Ibidem p. 100

[49] Ibid pp. 106-108 emphasis mine.

[50] How to understand and resolve very stressful emotions I have shown in detail in my previous book, here we look at other aspects of emotions.

[51] Santagati, Steve: "Mannual. So funktioniert der Mann." Fischer. 2010. S. 235

[52] Ibidem p. 286-287

[53] Ibidem p. 289

[54] Ibidem p. 288

[55] Hanson, Rick: Denken wie ein Buddha. Gelassenheit und innere Stärke durch Achtsamkeit. (Original title: Hardwiring Happiness). Heyne 2018. pp. 47-48. emphasis by Hanson.

[56] Ibid p. 51,50

[57] Ibidem p. 58-59

[58] Lyubomirsky, Sonja: Glücklich SEIN. Warum Sie es in der Hand haben, zufrieden zu leben. Campus 2013. p.121

[59] Ibidem p. 122

[60] Ibidem p. 129

[61] Ibid. S128

[62] Ibid p.130

[63] Brewer, Judson: Unwinding anxiety: new science shows how to break the cycles of worry and fear to heal your mind. Avery, Penguin Random House LLC, 2021. There is also an excellent app on this, which I can only recommend. So far only available in English and Spanish. (Translation from English by me.)

[64] Ibid. S.33

[65] Ibid. S.31

[66] De Mello. S. 85

[67] Hanson p.82

[68] Hanson p.82

[69] Ibidem p. 137

[70] There are many other ways to use this technique, including, for example, to counter negative feelings with positive ones that are appropriate and can resolve them. By appropriate is meant the context of the (unfulfilled) need. To see exactly how this works, I would refer you to Hanson's book. But even in my short example, you can see, for example, the feeling of connectedness, which may very well be an antidote to loneliness.

[71] Lyubomirsky, Glücklich SEIN. Warum Sie es in der Hand haben, zufrieden zu leben. Campus 2013.

[72] Ibid p.33

[73] Ibidem p. 34-35

[74] If you haven't seen them yet, I recommend the following documentaries: We Feed the World, Food Inc, Super Size Me 2: Holy Chicken! and Earthlings, although this is a very violent film.

[75] If not, then you are enlightened ;)

[76] Duhigg, Charles: Die Macht der Gewohnheit. Warum wir tun, was wir tun . Piper 2020. p. 144

[77] Tschechne, Rainer: Die Angst vor dem Glück. Warum wir uns selbst im Weg stehen. Herbig. 2012. p. 163.

[78] Ibidem p. 165

[79] Ibidem p. 223

[80] Ibidem p. 208

[81] Ibidem p. 215

[82] Duhigg. S. 74-78

[83] Ibid p. 92,79

[84] Ibidem p. 336 ff.

[85] Ibidem p. 118-119

[86] Ibidem p.173

[87] Thaler, Richard H.: Nudge. Nudge. Wie man kluge Entscheidungen anstößt. Ullstein 2020. p. 16

[88] Ricard, Matthieu: Glück. Knaur Mesnssana 2009. p. 270,281 emphasis mine.

[89] Ibidem p. 282

[90] Fredrickson, Barbara: Die Macht der guten Gefühle. Wie eine positive Haltung Ihr Leben dauerhaft verändert. Campus 2011.

[91] Ibid p. 27,26

[92] Ibidem p. 39

[93] You can test yours at the website posititvitiratio.com, Fredrickson recommends doing it daily for at least two weeks to get a meaningful average.

[94] Ibidem p. 186

[95] Fredrickson, Barbara: Love 2.0. Creating Happiness and Health in Moments of Connection. Plume (Penguin group) 2014.p. 4

[96] Ibidem p. 17

[97] Ibidem p. 36